I HOPE THE STARS

TAKE YOU BACK

A POETRY COLLECTION

By Lauren Levi

For mum, for everything.

For Kiria, for encouraging me to write again.

For Harriet, for helping me to find my voice.

I Hope The Stars Take You Back

I. LIFE

Travesty

If God is really omnipresent
then surely they are laughing with me.
Misfortunate and missed chances
are no stranger to me.
And I've lived more through my dreams
than in reality
that waking up has now become more of
a mere formality.

I ask my soul if she feels the same way
and she just shrugs at me.
Love feels like a lost melody
which doesn't make sense to me.
And it seems to me like a
tragedy — no, better yet, a travesty.
Like elastic bands around my heartstrings
just so I can breathe easily.

Stars

I tell my secrets to the stars,
my nightly company.
They don't talk much
but they always listen to me.

Heart on my sleeve

You say that I shouldn't wear my heart
on my sleeve — *it isn't this season's fashion.*
But I'd rather risk going against the norm
than to exist devoid of passion.

Take me back

And I stand at night
looking up at the sky,
hoping that the stars
will take me back when I die.

No man's land

And in the battle between
my heart and mind,
I stand here in the middle,
struggling to pick a side.

21 grams

If the weight of the human soul
is *only* 21 grams, then why,
some days, does it feel so heavy?
I may not have the strongest of bones
or the biggest of muscles, but, most days,
they're enough to carry me.

Seance

Life can be like a seance,
and I've met so many ghosts in my time.
They usually take the form of people
who are not meant to be mine.

Lauren Levi

Hell *(after Sylvia Plath in 'Dickinson')*

She said that to write poetry
you must be willing to go
all the way down to Hell.
And I think I've been there before,
that heat feels familiar,
I know it well.
If Heaven is anything, then
it exists in your memory,
and Hell must be when
you forget about me.

Company

I made friends with my demons,
to put it simply —
we once were enemies
but I now call them *'company'*.

Lauren Levi

Carry me

Even on the days I think I don't —
I truly love my body.
Because even after everyone else leaves,
she's always there to carry me.

Whole

I stay up late at night
writing poetry
in the hopes to fill the cracks
in my soul.
I have to say, to date,
it's going pretty great.
I'm starting to feel whole.

Lauren Levi

Human

We wrap our arms around each other
and push our hearts together to feel love.
We look up at the Gods and the stars
to seek our answers from above.
At night, we lie down, close our eyes
and practice death.
And when we get nervous,
we hold our breath.

When we get really sad,
we leak from our eyes.
And when one of us leaves —
we talk to the skies.

We try to heal our broken hearts with
fermented fruit, drugs and half written rhymes.
It can be a funny thing being
human sometimes.

Incantations

I whisper kind words like
incantations at night
in the hopes that I
might finally win this fight.
Because something will die
today, but it won't be me.
It will be my anger, my hate
and my negativity.

Perfect

If you be you
and I'll be me,
what a perfect place
this world could be.

Death

Death kindly tucks me in at night.
She places a kiss on my forehead
and promises that there are no longer
any monsters hiding underneath my bed.
And before she turns out the light,
she pulls me close, and holds me tight.
She said today was not my time to go —
but makes no promises for tomorrow.

Endless possibility

You say that you are not beautiful,
but I wish that you could see
that you are made of stardust
and *endless possibility*.

Agnostic

So now I lie awake at night
wondering if there is a God,
and I try to think positively.
In the hopes that there is
a father figure out there
who *actually* wants me.

Pain

She asked me why I write poetry and I said
because I don't know where else to put the hurt.
I can't leave it in my mind
and I can't bury it in the earth.
So I carve these words off my heart
and hope that one day,
someone looks at my pain
and calls it art.

A beautiful life

I'm not known for making things easy.
And I'm not the kind to easily let go.
So before she decides to come for me
there is something that she should know,
I'm going to live a beautiful life,
full of love and so much soul,
so that when Death finally comes for it
she will struggle to take it all.

One day

One day I'm going to buy
a big house by the coast,
invite the skeletons from my closet
and fill the rooms with ghosts.
Each night we will toast
to the end of our misery
and promise to *always*
keep each other company.

II. LOVE

Far away

You look at me and I'm
not quite sure what to say.
With you Heaven doesn't
feel too far away.

Lost souls

And we could stay
this way forever —
like lost souls
shipwrecked together.

Hope

I like to think that hope is
slow dancing in the kitchen at 3am,
and praying that in the next life
I get to love you all over again.

Jealous

I'm not a jealous person,
except for the times that I am.
And what I mean when I say that is,
I'm jealous of every person
in every moment with you
that I miss.

Arms

I don't go in search of butterflies anymore.
Instead, I look for safe. I look for calm.
Give me a book and a fireplace
and a safe space in your arms.

Lauren Levi

Worship

I say that I'm not sure what I believe in,
but I swear that when you touch my lips
my knees ache for the floor —
and this must be how it feels to worship.

Enough

I'll know it's love
because it will be tough,
when suddenly forever
doesn't feel enough.

Belief

I grew up believing that I would
never make it to Heaven.
Not holy enough to be let in.
But then I saw you.
And you looked at me.
And I found something to believe in.

Fate

I'm going to get into a bar fight
with fate just to have a little
more time with you.
I don't know who I'll be when it's
over, but I've always known how to
take a punch or two.

Forever

Let's do something crazy.
Like grow old together.
Let's show everyone
how to do forever.

Next to you

I'm not sure what my place is
here or if I truly have a part.
But standing here, next to you,
I think, is a really good start.

Home

Your skin feels like home,
and what I mean
when I say that is,
I could grow old in
your arms and stay
young with your kiss.

Starlit night

In another universe you say
'No, let's just be friends'
and nothing would begin
so nothing could really end.
But here we are, underneath
the same starlit night,
and you're holding my hand
and everything feels right.

Find each other

I'll bring you your favourite tea
every morning when you wake,
and we will always forgive each other
for our past mistakes.
At night we will watch meteors
fly across the midnight sky,
and promise to always find each other
— *even after we die.*

Slow burn

You're that type of
slow burn love.
The kind that I can
never get enough of.

Fear

I do not fear that much in life,
of this I know is true.
But the thought that keeps me up at night
is the fear of losing you.

Adore

And I guess what my words are trying to say
can now be summed up in a few —
so to cut to the chase and put it simply:
I adore you.

Chaos/calm

And just like the chaos that's found
only in the calm,
I dream I'm falling every night
but wake up safely in your arms.

Vanilla sky

Love to me looks like two people,
whiskey soaked and feeling high,
dancing in bare feet
underneath a vanilla sky.

Mine

I can learn to be patient.
I can truly learn to wait.
Because when you do find me,
I'll tell you that this was fate.

So I'll play out the long game.
and I'll wait out the time.
Until the day comes around
when I can finally call you
mine.

Insomniac

The moon is an insomniac —
but that's okay, because I am too.
The night has become a familiar friend
who I tell all about you.

A writer's love

I tell everyone that I want to
fall in love with a writer,
and they always ask me why.
I say because although I don't want to
live forever, a part of me
doesn't want to die.

Time in a bottle

If I could bottle this moment,
then I would only break it out
for special occasions.
I would label it with summer nights
crescent moons and never ending
constellations.

I would be sure to keep it on the top shelf
where all the good things are kept.
Low enough to touch,
yet high enough to feel infinite.

A bottle full of this moment of you and me
and everything we could hope to be.
It would have its own vintage —
and the year would be infinity

Sky dive

I don't just fall in love,
I actually sky dive.
It's the only time that falling
has ever made me feel alive.

Infinity

You.
Me.
And infinity.
The only forever
that I want to
see.

Truth

Truth be told, I've always felt
a bit strange in my body,
and I think it's because it
doesn't really belong to me.

Our bodies are on loan from the
earth and made from the stars,
and maybe that's why I feel you
wherever you are.

Epic love

I told everyone that I wanted
an *epic love*,
but I never knew what
it looked like.
And then along came you
and I thought
that maybe,
just maybe,
I might.

Don't

Don't promise me a forever
that you don't intend to see.
So don't tell me it's love
if you don't *really* want me.

Your kiss

I'm worried that anything else
will pale compared to this.
And that when someone else's lips
touch mine, I'll think about your kiss.

True

I don't know how else to say it,
what more could make it true?
I don't want anyone else,
I
    just
        want
           you.

III. HEARTBREAK

Like rain

I fell for you like rain —
but you carry an umbrella now.
I keep falling towards the canvas
and somehow still end up in
puddles on the ground.

And you walk on by
and leave me to drown.

And you'd have barely thought about it —
had it even crossed you mind?
That to be so blasé about our affections
is not how we're designed.
But you keep on walking and I pray
that you'll look back,
to the girl now lying on the cold tarmac.

B-side

My heart is a B-side of songs
that you would never listen to.
It's a cassette recording of scribbles
that I've lived my life through.

The tape has been pulled through
and wound back so many times
(some thought I was ruined —
but I knew that I'd be fine).

Almost

And I'll look for it again from
city to city and coast to coast,
but nothing will change the fact
that you were my favourite *almost*.

Survive

And just like the trees in the winter,
with their leaves amongst the snow,
I realise that in order to survive,
I must also learn how to let go.

Feeling

And tonight, I guess,
I miss you.
But please don't
ask me why.
I've tried to kill
the feeling,
but it doesn't
want to die.

Stranger

Sometimes it was easy,
but in the end, it was hard.
And now I'm just a stranger
who once lived in your heart.

Halfway

I ask you to meet me halfway
and you don't use your map
and lose your way.
And I keep waiting.
Five more minutes.
They're going to make it.
They still could.
But deep down I know
that if you really wanted to,
then you already would.

Jazz

If our final moments were a song
they would be smooth, soft, jazz.
And the melody would remind me
of the love that we once had.

Salvage

I don't think that I'll ever get used
to the absence that now lingers between us.
But maybe, in the wreckage of what we had,
I can *salvage* what is left of my trust.

Chance

I hope that we get the chance
to meet again one day,
when things don't feel so tough.
You'll wear your favourite dress
and I'll put my best foot forward,
and maybe, that will be enough.

Promise

No, love no longer exists
in the space between you and I.
Perhaps I'll find it again
with someone new.
I promise that I'll try.

Gracefully

I've always struggled to
walk away from things gracefully.
But maybe, *just this once*,
I'll do what's right for me.

Fairytales

And out of all the fairytales
that I ever believed —
my favourite story was the one
where you *didn't* leave.

Someone like you

I'm not sure what scares me most;
never finding someone like you,
or if the day comes when I
finally do.

Greek tragedy

And now when I think
about you and me —
every day it feels less
like a Greek Tragedy.

Salvageable parts

I had hoped that one day
we might upcycle my heart.
It's been broken before
but there's salvageable parts.

Easier

It gets easier each day without you
— but a part of me
                    doesn't want it to be.

Purgatory

It's one of the worst places to be,
trapped inside love's purgatory.
Am I a lover still or am I now a friend?
Is this the beginning or is this the end?

Blue

I'm afraid that the person I am now
is a pale shade of blue.
Nowhere near as colourful
as who I was with you.

North Star

I thought that you were my North Star
and that you would finally guide me home.
But when the sun rose and all was said and done
— I realised that I was on my own.

In between times

I hope that you think of me when the
sun sets and the moon is yet to rise,
because those were my favourite moments,
my favourite in between times.
Instead of when you couldn't decide,
whether to love me or leave me behind.

Seams

"It burns," I said.
She asked me "What do you mean?"

"The feeling of you unloving me
pulls me apart at the seams."

Highs

She gave me the highest of highs
and the lowest of lows.
More addictive than any drug
that I've ever known.

Ugly

I almost destroyed
the beautiful parts of me,
for someone who could
only see the ugly.

One-sided love

On the days where 'I miss you'
threatens to fall from my mouth
and my fingers itch for the phone,
I try my best to remember that
being in a one-sided love
is no better than being alone.

Universes

If there are infinite universes
then perhaps one exists where
you did not break my heart.
But I'm not there and you're
not here. So I guess we're
still living worlds apart.

Simple

You and me
were supposed to be
as simple as this
poetry.

Colours (*after Halsey*)

I met a girl whose love was blue,
and for her mine burnt red.
Together we made purple —
but she wanted something else instead.

So I made my love turn white,
it no longer burned like fire.
I became everything she wanted
just to be the one that she desired.

And then she met a girl whose love
was yellow — and I felt mine turn green.
And now I'm sat here on my own —
pulling blue out of my dreams.

Memories

At night, ghosts aren't
what haunt me.
Instead of spirits
it's our memories.

Depths

The past is always present
when I think of you.
I dive into the depths of our memories
with rocks in my shoes.
The weight of it all pulls me down
and I wonder why I always drown.

Ricochet

Your tongue is like a *trigger*,
therefore your words must be *bullets*.
No wonder I felt the *ricochet*
through my heart when you *pulled* it.

Lauren Levi

Prestige

I stopped believing in magic
when I put my love in your hat,
and you made it disappear,
but you never brought it back.

Pillow talk

I still have the pillow that you bought that time,
but it no longer rests you head.
It's strange how small things can remind me
that you now sleep in someone else's bed.

Shatter

I watch the rain pour
and shatter on the ground,
and wonder why heartbreak
doesn't make a sound.

Pressure

They say it takes around
seven hundred and forty pounds to
split the average human's ribs apart.
So tell me, love, why did you
apply so much pressure
to my heart?

Lauren Levi

Heartache

Heartache is a funny thing
because I can't seem to cure the pain,
every time someone tries
to mention your name.

Shards

I'm still pulling shards of you
out of my broken heart,
and you're already finding
another to fill my part.

Hold on

Even after all this time
pain is all that I have left of you.
I hope that one day I can find
something else to hold on to.

Spaces

Grief now occupies where you once
lay on the left side of the bed,
and the spaces that you once filled
inside of my head.

Silent movies

Our memories replay like
silent movies on a screen,
and I always hope for a
different ending for me.

Memory lane

Co-star told me not to go
to Memory Lane today,
and it's as if they were aware,
that I would sit and wait
on that lonely road in the
hopes to meet you there.

Grief

My love is a runaway
who now lives on the street.
She cut her hair and changed
her name to 'Grief'.

Heaven's gate

I'm scared that if I'm the
first to get to Heaven's gate,
that I'll just sit down
for you and wait.

Letting go

I always think that letting go
is like performing a trust fall
with fate.
I only hope that this time
she doesn't reach for me
too late.

Out of reach

More than nothing,
less than something,
out of reach it seems.

Now I lie awake
just to avoid seeing
you in my dreams.

IV. RECOVERY

Discovery

In losing you
I became me.
So I guess a loss
became a discovery.

Lauren Levi

Bones

On the days where
every breath feels like lead,
and my demons wage
their wars inside of my head,
I know that there is hope
lining the walls of these bones.
I know that one day recovery
will welcome me home.

Muscle memory

I've had my heart broken
so many times before,
so it makes sense to me,
that healing has become
like second nature —
a muscle memory.

Recovery

My story is no longer sad
since healing finally came.
No one walks through recovery
and ever comes out the same.

Longest road

Recovery is the longest road
that I have ever walked.
And it began when I gave words
to my pain — and talked.

Some days

Some days I am more
full stop than semi colon;
more giving up that
just holding on.

Some days I am more
sunshine than rain.
More slowly healing
than in pain.

Coming home

I think I'm becoming who I'm meant to be,
I'm finally coming into my own.
I've been walking this road for so long now,
it finally feels like I'm coming home.

Lauren Levi

Anxiety

Let me tell you, anxiety is not being scared
of the monster from underneath your bed.
It's the adrenaline surge of battling the
demons who now occupy your head.
And now they're calling out for blood.
They say they're not leaving without a war.
Some days, I turn up ready for battle,
and others, I don't know what my sword is for.

Acceptance

Waiting taught me that you're not
trying to make your way back to me.
Acceptance finally taught me that
I wouldn't want you to be.

Wanted

I've betrayed myself so many times
that there's now wanted posters hanging
inside of my mind.
And the reward for my capture is serenity,
my own inner peace.
Because when it comes to my happiness,
I am my own thief.

Glad

You cannot lose something
that you never really had.
So when they tell me that
you're happy now —
I say that I'm glad.

Lauren Levi

Post-break up to do list

Unlearn your love language
to seek other tongues,
give back the air you
breathed into my lungs.
Pack up your clothes
but keep my favourite tee,
and try not to wonder
if you still think of me.
Give back the knife you
lodged deep in my back,
is this how it feels to have
an anxiety attack?
Take back my courage,
but give back your blame.
Remember that two people
don't heal the same.

Thrive

You said that without you
I wouldn't survive.
Now I imagine your face
as you watch me thrive.

Hero

In the story
of the battle
for my mental health,
I became my hero
because I chose
to save myself.

Sunrise

And after every heartbreak,
the sun always rises —
and I'm so grateful,
because she's always there
to pull me up
when I feel unable.

Lauren Levi

Sweet heart

I have a sweet heart
even though it's suffered before.
Because every time it breaks
it asks me how to love more.

Toxic

I have been toxic.
I can say that with
honesty.
But I work everyday
to be a better version
of me.
And ever since learning
all about recovery,
I vowed never to go back
to being the person
who poisoned me.

ABOUT THE AUTHOR

Lauren Levi is a British LGBT poet who calls Birmingham home.

Her poetry explores the highs of love, the lows of heartbreak and the beauty of recovery.

This is her first collection of poetry made available to the public.

You can follow Lauren on instagram @mslevi_ for regular poems.

Printed in Great Britain
by Amazon

79324204R00079